AN ORDINARY GUY'S GUIDE FOR LIFE

A philosophy for life
developed by Jason Hapstak

ISBN 978-1-63525-402-0 (Paperback)
ISBN 978-1-63525-403-7 (Digital)

Christian Faith Publishing, Inc.
296 Chestnut Street
Meadville, PA 16335
www.christianfaithpublishing.com

Printed in the United States of America

PREFACE

All thoughts in this book are my own personal thoughts. I don't read books, magazines, or any original literature, with the exception of pharmacy literature. If my thoughts are similar to any published thoughts or documents, I can assure you that I didn't steal your ideas.

I am a thirty-eight-year-old pharmacist. I am a married Roman Catholic with two kids. I have rescued numerous animals from humane societies. I don't belong to any organizations, clubs, or associations. I watch TV, movies, documentaries, and sports. I hate social media. I am a religious person but not necessarily sold on all aspects of religion. I play sports and enjoy nature. All thoughts included in this book are a compilation of things I've seen, experienced, contemplated, and interpreted for myself.

CHAPTER ONE

The Origin

No matter what religion a person believes in, there has to be a grand creator of the universe. I call him/her God. God is not someone we can understand. God is everything there ever was, is, and will be. God was here before there was time. God created all building blocks of life and therefore enabled life itself, in all forms, in every part of the universe. Here is why there has to be a God: because you are here right now reading this. Did you just spontaneously appear, or did you get here because life evolved over millions and billions of years from elemental molecules to single proteins to complex multicelled organisms? If you have parents and grandparents or ancestors of any sort, that question is answered.

If the big bang theory is correct, which basically states that the universe was created from an explosion of a "God particle," which gives mass and energy to everything in the universe, then the entire universe originated from one point. Since the universe is still expanding, as evidenced by the fact of the red outlines that distant galaxies have, we can safely say that it is moving outward from an original point. The red outline of a distant galaxy means that it is moving away from us, or losing energy. If a galaxy had a blue outline, it means that the galaxy is coming toward us and increasing in energy. Considering the spectrum of light, red waves have less energy than blue waves.

In addition, let's assume that the theory that energy can neither be created nor destroyed but can only change forms is also correct. This theory holds up only if we assume that the original energy, or creation energy, was in fact made. At the beginning of time, the God particle had to have been created by the Grand Architect of all things and this particle contained all of the energy that the universe would ever contain.

Quantum physicists might argue that there are some theoretical subatomic particles that can spontaneously appear and therefore, some elemental building blocks of life may have just appeared randomly out of nowhere. However, if these random particles possess any sort of energy, then the constant energy theory would dictate that they must have come from somewhere else or some other form of energy. This argument can go around and around, and the truth is no one living will ever know, nor will anyone be able to prove with 100 percent accuracy how everything got started. The reality is that it comes down to faith and logic. Before there was anything, there had to be something. That something, I believe, was God, the Creator.

God was here before time when there was nothing, and God decided to somehow create the building blocks of life. If the building blocks of life weren't created, then none of this would be possible. In my opinion, it is illogical to think that from nothing in the beginning, a particle randomly appeared without intervention from anyone or anything, which would eventually give rise to everything in the universe. This is why I feel that atheism is also illogical. In my opinion, being an atheist is an act of laziness because saying that you don't believe in a creator or god of any sort is just an excuse to not be accountable for your actions or examine yourself and explore what it really means to be alive.

CHAPTER TWO

Are We Alone?

When the big bang occurred at the beginning of time, the universe started expanding. All matter in the universe, and therefore all the building blocks of life, emerged from one place. We can say with 100 percent certainty that life is on Earth. Earth was lucky enough for atoms to bond and become molecules, which would combine to form proteins, which would aggregate and give rise to single-celled organisms, and after a few billion rounds of evolution, here we are, reading this paragraph.

The question really shouldn't be "are we alone?" but rather "where else is life?" It is naïve and illogical to think that life is only located on one planet, because it would mean that even though the entire universe started from a single point and theoretically every-place in the universe had the same chances of receiving the correct building blocks and chemicals for life, only Earth was blessed enough to have life evolve. Conditions in other places might be different, but it doesn't mean that life can't start. For example, here on Earth, we have both extreme heat and extreme cold, and we have found bacteria living in both of these places, which we previously thought were impossible to sustain life. I think that finding life on other planets is more of a detection problem rather than an absence of life.

The first problem is that we don't even know what is in the universe yet. By this I mean that we aren't even sure how many galaxies there are. More specifically, we don't even know what is in our own Milky Way galaxy yet. We can't see the far reaches of space yet, so we don't know what is out there. The second problem is that we can't travel to these distant places yet to search for life. The third problem is that life on other planets may not require the same living conditions as Earth. We may search other solar systems for evidence of water because on Earth all life needs water. However, life in other places may not need water to survive, and therefore if you search the galaxy for only this substance, the search is too narrow, and life won't be found. The fourth problem is that life outside of Earth may be beyond our sensory capacity and technological capability to detect. By this I mean that our senses or technology on the space vessel isn't capable of detecting or visualizing what is there. For example, we can't see bacteria without the help of magnifying devices, but bacteria are everywhere and very much alive. If life on another planet exists in an area of the visual field which our eyes or instruments can't detect, we would not see what is there. Extrapolating on this, no one knows what conditions exist in the far reaches of space or what instruments are required to detect foreign life, and therefore, we could easily miss seeing life in other places. All of these factors make it unlikely that we will detect life elsewhere anytime soon, but that doesn't mean that there isn't life anywhere else.

CHAPTER THREE

Do We Have Anyone Helping Us?

If we assume that there is in fact life in other parts of the universe, what does that mean for us here on Earth? I believe that life as we know it is the result of having been visited by travelers from other places both in the past and even right now. In ancient times, we might have called them angels, gods, or people from the stars, and in modern times, we would call them aliens. The best evidence that we have been visited by people or beings from other worlds in the past is the architecture built by ancient cultures, such as the Egyptian pyramids, Indian and Chinese temples, and other megalithic structures including the Stonehenge and the moai of Easter Island.

How did people much less technologically advanced than us today build structures which we can't recreate now? How did these ancient people acquire so much knowledge about the constellations and astrological navigation? How did our ancient ancestors build such immense structures which happen to align perfectly with the four cardinal directions and other important constellations, such as Orion or Sirius, during specific times of the year? I believe that they had guidance. Quite honestly, the pieces just don't fit unless we assume that they had help from a more advanced civilization. In fact, since we can't find the tools used to build these structures, we don't know how they moved these thousand-ton blocks into place, and we don't know how such precise cuts in stone could have been made, we must postulate that the required skills and technology was acquired from outside of Earth.

When we consider trying to navigate or perform orientation using the stars, we realize that is not an easy task today even with modern technology. It seems more plausible that someone with intricate knowledge of the stars taught this skill to a less advanced species rather than a less advanced people learning it on their own. In modern times, we went from riding around on horses to walking on the moon in less than a hundred years. We went from using telegraphs and Morse code to using smartphones, which can do basically everything now, due to the invention of the transistor. Why, or rather how, did we achieve such technological breakthroughs in such a short amount of time? If the simplest explanation is often the correct one, then, in all cases, we were most likely helped by someone with superior knowledge as compared to stumbling onto the solution randomly.

I must thank the show *Ancient Aliens* and in particular Erich von Daniken and Giorgio Tsoukalos for exposing this possibility to me, but what if all of the ancient carvings, statues, drawings, and written descriptions of strange people worshiped as gods weren't just artists being creative but an actual depiction of who was there? These depictions and descriptions are all over the world in numerous cultures. There are ancient texts such as Egyptian hieroglyphs, Indian Sanskrit such as the Mahabharata and the Ramayana, and Sumerian cuneiform describing the visitors and how they got here. Expanding on this, what if the ancient Roman, Greek, Indian, and Norse gods also existed? Why would ancient cultures devote so much time and energy creating likenesses of these gods and building temples in their honor unless they were critically important to them?

The possibility exists that the ancient people created all of these deities to explain things that they couldn't explain, such as life, death, lightning, thunder, and other natural phenomenon. However, we can't go back in time to ask these people why they offered so much devotion, and detail, to these ancient gods. It seems to make more sense, to me at least, that less intellectual and less advanced cultures would worship something concrete and plausible, maybe something that they had seen with their own eyes, as compared to something abstract. They would most likely have worshipped someone who helped shape their community by teaching them how to build, how to navigate, and how to perhaps survive. For these reasons, I believe that all of the ancient gods were here on earth at some time, and the ancient depictions and descriptions of these visitors were not just figments of an artist's imagination. Perhaps we already have the hard evidence we need that we aren't alone.

Allowing ourselves to believe that ancient gods existed and that our ancient ancestors had help from extraterrestrial visitors does not in any way diminish God. The reason for this is because God, the Divine Creator, created all building blocks for life, and therefore enabled life itself, in all forms, in every part of the universe. Everything in existence throughout the universe owes its existence to God. Believing in extraterrestrials and alien life only adds to the phenomenal array of life throughout the universe that God created.

I think that it is more important to ask "why does anyone outside of earth help us?" rather than "who exactly helped us?" There is certainly a history of people on Earth being helped or guided throughout time. In addition to the extraterrestrial travelers who might have helped shape early society, there is also the belief that our deceased loved ones can still interact and be present in our lives, perhaps as guardian angels, shielding us from harm. In the Bible, numerous other angels have been mentioned, such as those that are said to have stopped Abraham from sacrificing his son Isaac to God and the angel Gabriel who is said to have given Mary, the mother of Jesus, the divine news that she is pregnant with the Son of God. Angels are also believed to help take the soul from this life to the next.

Throughout time, we have been assisted and guided by those whose true identity remains unknown. It is important to realize that what they have done for us in the past and continue to do for us today is what really matters as compared to defining who or what an angel is or even who or what an ancient god or extraterrestrial visitor is. I believe that we as humans don't possess the ability to know or capacity to understand the workings of God and the universe, and perhaps this is why we don't know, at least in this life, the identity of our helpers.

Perhaps the reason why the people of Earth get help from beyond Earth can be explained by the fact that creatures of Earth help each other. What if the universal law of our Creator is to help one another? There are millions of examples in both the human and animal world of one individual helping another. There are symbiotic relationships whereby one organism survives off of another so that both can thrive, such as sharks, which provide protection, and gobies, which clean parasites off of the shark. There are parental relationships whereby a species might care for an individual of either the same or different species due to the parents of the individual being abandoned or killed, such as with elephant seals adopting orphaned pups or mother dogs adopting kittens. There are also what I call altruistic, or Good Samaritan, relationships whereby one individual helps another just because they need help, such as a person volunteering at a homeless shelter.

The examples are too numerous to define, but perhaps, in much the same nature as a person cares for a pet, species from outside our planet feel the need to help us. It doesn't make much sense for a more advanced species, which doesn't need assistance to survive and is capable of eradicating a less advanced species, to provide help, guidance, and companionship unless it is ingrained in their nature. If we look at it this way, it begins to become clear that angels, gods, and extraterrestrials have guided and protected us throughout time because we are all created by the Divine Creator and the capacity and obligation to help others is embedded in our DNA.

CHAPTER FOUR

The Afterlife

A person's spirit can be called many things, such as a soul, an essence, even a personality. It encompasses all of the behaviors, characteristics, beliefs, and thoughts that one has. Whatever it is called, it is the driving life force that makes each life unique. Intentionally, I say *each life unique* because I believe that everything which is alive has a spirit. With people, it is obvious that different personalities and driving forces exist, not only across cultures, but within families. No two people are alike, and even twins have unique personalities.

However, if we look close enough at other species, we can see the uniqueness of each individual in that species too. Pet owners will say that their dog or cat is one of a kind, maybe because their dog howls in a bizarre way when petted or because their cat likes to sleep in bizarre places. More unique pet owners might say that their reptile likes to get a bath or that their rabbit likes to watch TV. Venturing out further, even wild animals like elephants can recognize themselves in a mirror, indicating that they consider themselves a separate entity from other elephants.

Whatever the species, unique characteristics are present, and it just takes keen observation to notice the personality or spirit within. Therefore, I'm suggesting that if something is alive, it has an energy unique to itself. This energy is what makes every life special.

Many religions believe that after life on earth is over, something happens to the spirit of the individual. From a scientific point of view, the energy which drives a life (their spirit or soul) must go somewhere after that life is over if it is true that energy can neither be created nor destroyed. One can say that when something dies, the energy which drove their life is now fueling the decomposition process. I disagree with this because it isn't really their spiritual energy or essence which is providing the fuel but rather their remains which provide the building blocks and food sources for other organisms to live.

So what happens to the life energy, or spirit, after death? In my opinion, it seems logical that the unique energy which drives every individual on earth maintains itself, somehow, and gets cycled through death into an afterlife. As mystical as it may seem, it is the reverse process of how that energy originally arrived here. If the soul can arrive at conception or birth, then it can also depart at death. With this life cycle, or energy cycle, in mind, the next question to ask is where the soul goes after death.

Essentially, an afterlife is the belief that after the soul dies on earth, it lives on somewhere else. Religions may support reincarnation, purgatory, heaven, hell, or a combination of these. People that have had near-death experiences often tell of a bright, warming light, an extreme peace, seeing their life flash before their eyes, or a communication with someone who previously died. These examples may give us a glimpse of what the afterlife is like. It is not surprising to me that many of the stories are similar. However, these were near-death experiences, not death experiences. No one has ever died and come back to tell what the afterlife is actually like.

I am not discrediting near-death experiences in any way. I believe that what happened in each case was real, and it would be glorious if the afterlife was like what they experienced. I think that many near-death experiences are similar because the brain behaves in a certain way to comfort every individual as the soul moves temporarily back and forth from earth to wherever it is going. My point is that I believe that every death experience and final destination of the soul is as unique as the soul itself. For this reason, I don't believe that there is a singular heaven, hell, purgatory, or reincarnation. If no two individuals are exactly alike, then no two individuals can have the same afterlife.

Throughout life, an individual will encounter good and evil. What if heaven is a place where someone can see all of the good that occurred throughout their life and hell is a place where they can see all of the evil throughout their life? My concept of heaven and hell is not the traditional one where heaven is a paradise and hell is a raging, tortuous inferno for the damned. I think that for heaven to be a heaven, it has to be perfect for each individual soul and, therefore, can't just be located in a singular location. I also just can't imagine that a divine creator who would create the universe and allow for all life in all forms would also create a place so horrible that it would need to be ruled by a supreme evil leader.

I think that our Creator is what good is. Good is hope, happiness, caring, and compassion. Good is acting with these virtues in mind. Good is an idea to strive for, a challenge to be to the best that we can be. Evil, on the other hand, is the absence of good. Evil is acting with cruelty, hatred, and disdain. Evil is the result of not caring for or respecting life. Evil is the result of free will and choices. Therefore, evil wasn't created by our Creator; it was chosen by those who live as a result of free will.

When someone dies and their spirit moves on, I believe that they are faced with the choices they made in life. Our good choices are seen as the purest form of good, a paradise of sorts. We can see love and kindness in every possible way, maybe in the form of loved ones, loved places, or loved experiences. All of the good in life, we see in our heaven. Conversely, I also believe that we must face our evil acts as well. These evil acts might appear as tortures or horrible visions, the purest form of evil, a hell of sorts. All of the evil in life, we see in our hell. We come face to face with our own demons.

Perhaps purgatory is a place where we get to think about our life on earth and learn from our mistakes. Purgatory is neither a heaven nor a hell but rather a contemplation area void of distractions. Sometimes, we may get another chance at life on earth in some capacity in the form of reincarnation. Although the details elude me, reincarnation seems to be a sort of do-over, a reset button pushed by our Creator with a new game ahead and a chance to get it right this time. Heaven and hell are concepts that we will never understand and, quite frankly, aren't meant to understand.

There is no one that can say for sure that they have it figured out, and this is the way it is. There are no experts on this subject. Your opinion is just as correct as my opinion. My idea of the afterlife may be completely wrong, but I'm not going to change the way that I live my life. I do the best that I can every day of my life to be the best person I can be for myself, others, and all forms of life. Maybe when my spirit leaves this earth (and it has to go somewhere), I will get to experience the choices I make in life. I want to make those choices that are good for others and avoid the evil choices. Even if I'm wrong about heaven and the afterlife and there is nothing after death, at least the people still living can say, "Wow, he was a kind man that did everything he could for others," and I would know in the end that I did my best. However, if there really is an afterlife, is it worth taking the chance of being evil?

CHAPTER FIVE

Different Forms of the Afterlife

I believe that we see all of the good we did in life in our heaven, maybe in the form of loved ones, loved places, or loved experiences. However, what if our loved ones are still living? Does this mean that we have to wait for their death to be with them again? Can a soul pass from the afterlife back to some sort of life on earth? In my experience, the answer is yes. In my own life, whenever someone special to me has died, both animal and human, in some form or another, they have always come back to me to let me know that they are all right.

For example, when my great-aunt died, she made her presence known to me by preventing me from getting into a major accident right by my house. I was at an intersection, and my light had just turned green. As I started to go through the intersection, my foot got stuck under the accelerator, and I stopped halfway. At that moment, a car blew through their red light, narrowly avoiding me. Just as all of this was happening, she appeared to me for just a moment and said, "I'm OK, and you're OK." From that moment on, I knew she was happy and alive someplace else.

In another example, when my dalmatian suddenly had a massive spinal stroke and we were forced to put him to sleep because he was paralyzed from the neck down, I was devastated for weeks. I literally lay on my couch, in a dark silence, thinking about death and how this could possibly happen to such a strong, young dog. At that time, I was in college studying to be a veterinarian. As I lay there thinking about him, I realized, through his death, that my career path was not right for me. As much as I loved animals, I would never be able to put one to sleep. From that moment on, I changed my career path, and that is why I am a pharmacist today. My dog just kept appearing to me over and over in that dark silence, asking me, "Can you really handle being a vet?" It was on that couch that I learned about death and developed my whole philosophy on the afterlife. I realized that he must be OK and in a better place now if he is helping me make career choices.

Lastly, I wonder if it's a coincidence that whenever something good or funny happens that my grandmother would enjoy, the number 318 appears somewhere, maybe on a clock or timer. My grandmother lived at 318 Theodore Street for over eighty years.

My point to these stories is that when someone dies, to me, they aren't totally gone. They are still with us, somehow, someway, and we just have to be open to seeing them. It might take months or years. It might happen in a dream or in reality. It might even happen through someone else, such as a medium, who I believe are just more open to the signs than some people. My experiences are my own proof that the afterlife is real and that those who died aren't really gone. To the skeptic, I offer this question: Have you really been open enough in life to see the signs that your loved ones want you to see?

My personal experiences are just part of the total picture of the afterlife. They illustrate that once life on earth is over, there is still a way for our loved ones to communicate. Reincarnation, whereby the spirit or essence of someone who died gets another chance at life on earth in some capacity, may also be a way to explain how a soul's energy isn't lost at death. Whether it is their choice or our Creator's choice is unknown, and we aren't allowed to know if we are a reincarnation or not. If we remember who we were in a previous life, then we couldn't really live a reincarnated life as the same person, because we wouldn't have truly died. In addition, maybe we get our second chance in a totally different form, such as someone who loved water getting a chance as a fish or someone who hated snakes getting a chance to live as a serpent.

Reincarnation may be a concept created by man, but I still believe in it because I feel that we aren't meant to understand this whole process. If you live your whole life knowing that you get a strike two, would you really do your best in the first life? However, there may be some proof of reincarnation when we get a glimpse of a previous life, maybe in the form of a fleeting image or situation that may seem familiar, that we can't explain. Maybe the fact that some people say that they found their soul mate in this life is evidence that they were somehow connected in a previous life.

Whatever the case may be, all we can really say is that we have our life on earth now and someone gave it to us. Is our current life the result of our Creator giving someone a second chance, or is each life one and done? We aren't meant to understand this process, and we can never prove it one way or the other, but if we are faced with the good and evil we do during life before an afterlife is determined, then we should do our best with the life we have now.

Just as there are gray areas in life, I think that there are gray areas in the afterlife. The afterlife gray area is the theory of ghosts. Maybe purgatory is the realm of ghosts? Maybe ghosts don't quite get a second chance at life in the form of reincarnation or reach their heaven because they need some time to ponder their choices on earth. Whatever the case may be, some people think that the concept of ghosts is ridiculous, while others that have seen them strongly disagree. I believe that ghosts are possible, and more importantly, I believe that if they are here, then they are here for a purpose. Their purpose on earth is not for the living to understand, and we should respect their time here and not try to exploit it.

After we die, the energy of our life goes somewhere. Depending on our choices in life, we might get to dwell in our heaven and interact with our loved ones for all eternity, get a second chance at life in the form of reincarnation, or get stuck somewhere in between in the realm of purgatory and ghosts. What we do in life determines our eternity.

CHAPTER SIX

The Origin of Evil

I don't believe in a singular hell or the devil, and I think that free will is what created evil. With every choice in life, we can go in one of two directions—the good and righteous path or the dark and evil road. Every time that we choose the latter, our personal demon gets stronger. If we are faced with all of the evil that we caused in life after our death, we are essentially confronting our demons when we die. The stronger the demon, the more hellish and torturous the afterlife will seem. Lucifer, the guardian of personal hell, makes sure that we encounter the demons which we created throughout life. All of the betrayals, meanness, cruelty, and pain we caused others becomes personified. However, I believe that God gives us the chance to vanquish the demons by truly feeling sorry for the evil deeds committed and atoning for them. Just as free will led to evil choices, God, in His loving mercy, lets us choose if we want to crush the demon we created.

Although I don't believe in a supreme demon, the devil, I do believe in Lucifer, the fallen angel. The devil, I believe, was created by man to give evil a face. Evil is very real but abstract, so it needed something concrete for people to visualize, fear, and hopefully avoid, which is why pictures and paintings of the devil are so horrific. Lucifer, however, is very real. I often wonder if Lucifer fell from God's grace and was forced to rule over personal hells or voluntarily left to perform the function. It actually comes down to a matter of translation of ancient texts and what it means to fall.

For example, was it a forced fall or a voluntary fall? A forced fall would imply a removal from heaven, while a voluntary fall implies self-sacrifice to complete a job. If we consider the Apostle's Creed—which is a Roman Catholic prayer that states that after Jesus died, He descended into hell before He rose from the dead—and if we consider in the Book of Revelation, whereby Jesus tells John that He has the keys to death and the netherworld, we see that Lucifer has a relationship with Jesus. Lucifer must respect and abide by the rules that Jesus set forth for the dead and those in hell facing their demons. I find it unlikely that a rebellious angel would listen to the decrees of Jesus the Savior.

I find it more likely that Lucifer is actually an angel who listens to the Lord and performs a most undesirable task. More importantly, this is a crucial job because it is through reflection and analysis of a life lived that we see the consequences of our choices and face the music, and Lucifer is the one playing the song. In order to kill the demon which we created, atonement must occur and Lucifer must be convinced that we are truly sorry and the demon is dead, never to return again. In a way, Lucifer is actually the gatekeeper between our heaven and our hell. For this reason, I believe that Lucifer is actually an angel who evaluates a soul's true nature and intention, and this job can't be done by an agent of evil.

During our lifetime, we have the choice to let the demon live or to not even let it be born. We can make changes in our life to not let the demon gain power, because whether it is in this life or the next, we will have to face our demons.

CHAPTER SEVEN

The Institution of Marriage

By far, the hardest voluntary choice that you will ever have to make is the decision whether or not to get married. Life will present you with many different horrible and dilemma-ridden situations, and I'm keeping those choices separate from a choice that you traditionally make when happy. Marriage isn't just about love; it's about sharing a life. The life that you had before getting married is not the life you will have after saying the two little words "I do." When you utter those words, "I" becomes "we," and every decision that you make, till death or divorce do you part, affects the both of you.

When you decide to get married, and perhaps for years afterward, the passion that you feel for each other is intense and spectacular! You love the way the other person looks, and you can't keep your hands off of each other. You can't wait to see your better half and want to spend every moment together! In your eyes, your partner can do no wrong. Maybe you'll be lucky, and this passion won't ever cease, and you'll be in the honeymoon phase forever, but most of the time, the vacation will end. Marriage goes from play to work. Looks will fade, sex will cease, and little quirks that a person has becomes huge annoyances. Little tasks like taking out the trash, emptying the dishwasher, or putting the toilet paper on the dispenser in the correct orientation become huge issues. You go from can't waiting to see each other to hiding in a man cave or girl cove. Make no mistake about it, marriage is a job with a never-ending shift. However, I encourage everyone to do it.

When you enter into that sacred bond, you give up part of yourself. You enter into a covenant to be less selfish and pledge your life to another. In my opinion, it is a rite of passage to being a man or a woman. In much the same way that a high school boy has to try football, a premed student has to take organic chemistry (useless), or a medical resident has to work ridiculously long hours, to be in the club, you have to do it. You might think that as a bachelor, when you sleep with a lot of women, you are "the man!" This is not true—you are a boy until you get married. Boys have no loyalty or sense of commitment or self-sacrifice, while a man has these qualities. I don't have a similar reference for a girl, but my point is that marriage is the hardest job you will ever have with the greatest reward—a life-long partner.

Marriages, unfortunately, don't always work, and that is OK. Sometimes divorce is the only answer to irreconcilable differences or unforgivable acts. However, don't consider yourself to have lived a full life until you have fully committed yourself to someone else. This also applies to those who can't find that special someone or for those who can't get married, such as priests or nuns. Commit and give of yourself fully to your passion or your pets in order to get the most out of life. It isn't necessarily the act of marriage which is the rite of passage to manhood or womanhood, but rather the act of devoting one's life to their true calling.

It would certainly be nice if both players in a marriage were winners, but in every contest, there has to be a winner and a loser. However, this is not what marriage is about, as the best possible outcome is a tie. When one member of a marriage thinks that they are winning, such as when a man utters the words *happy wife, happy life*, the other member must theoretically think that they are losing, right? This is not the case at all, but the loser would want the winner to think this way.

The reason is that the energy which the losing partner previously used on himself, which the winner believes she has usurped and every whim that she has will now be acted upon by him for her pleasure, doesn't really get diverted to her. If we think of the law of conservation of energy, whereby energy cannot be created or destroyed but can only change forms, we will see that a man's passion for his own pleasures doesn't get destroyed, it just changes forms. Whether he admits it or not, every man will have a secret desire or passion which will be either unknown or at best mildly known to his partner.

It doesn't necessarily have to be sexual in nature; it can be a hobby, a pastime, or even a food he likes. For example, a man may play fantasy football, and his wife will probably be aware of this, but what she won't know is how much he craves playing and winning and feeling the power of managing a team or beating his friends. Perhaps this is one of the reasons why fantasy sports have become so popular! Another example is that a man may go fishing every Sunday but his wife won't know how much hunting and catching that monster fish excites him.

Guys must not be naive either, because the exact same thing happens with women. *Happy man, happy span*, as in *span of life*, is just as deceptive as *happy wife, happy life*. These are the reasons why there can't be a perceived winner and a loser in a marriage. If there really is a winner and a loser, the loser will be absolutely miserable, and the marriage won't work. If neither side will give an inch, there will be gridlock, and both parties will be miserable and eventually divorce. The only answer to marriage is a tie. Nobody wins, but everyone is happy or at least content.

Compromise is the fast track to achieving this. With compromise, you may have to give a little, but it is better than getting nothing at all. In addition, compromise must be used prudently; that is, choose your battles. Is it really worth having a negotiation over a brand of ketchup, or would it be wiser to deliberate over the type of car to buy? Is it worth fighting over who loads the dishwasher when you know that you like it done in a particular way? Is it easier to yell over leaving the lights on or to just shut them off yourself? Some items in a marriage are just quirks that you have to accept about the other person, and there is little to no use in fighting or negotiating over them.

Marriage is a journey, not a destination. Enjoy the exploration because each day is an adventure down an unknown river. I don't have all of the answers; in fact, I barely have any. I am working each day to figure out the correct path. At this point in my life, I realize that not talking, holding grudges, going to bed angry, not asking questions, and refusing to be vulnerable only make my life suck worse compared to making her feel bad for some wrong I feel that she inflicted upon me. I also know, however, that the good days and great times erase all of the bad ones. I am working on being more accepting and realizing that I can't change the opinions or behaviors of my partner, but I can try to understand them and deal with what is in a manner that I find bearable. I try to handle the holding-a-grudge and going-to-bed-angry issues by asking myself, "If I were to die tomorrow, would I be proud of the way that I acted today?" Almost always, I answer that question with "no, I would be ashamed of how I acted today," but one must process anger and grant forgiveness before taking the next step.

Forgiveness, when you really think about it, is actually a selfish practice because when you forgive, you aren't actually excusing the behavior of the offending individual, but rather not allowing the act to dominate and consume all of your mental energy. The same holds true for anger. It drains one mentally, but what good does it really do? With forgiveness and letting go of anger comes mental freedom and clarity. As far as refusing to be vulnerable, which is difficult when you envision yourself as the protector and defender, you have to realize that letting your guard down is what leads to intimacy and trust. If the other person is only used to dealing with the battle-hardened shell of the partner, then you never get to truly know the other person. In summary, my three keys to marriage are forgiveness, acceptance, and compromise.

CHAPTER EIGHT

The Blessing of Kids

Even though I might know the keys to marriage, being married is not easy, and sometimes kids are the saving grace which holds a marriage together until the couple finds some common ground. However, raising a child is also quite difficult, but the rewards far outweigh the demands. Once you get past the first year, where basically your job as a parent is to keep your infant alive and healthy, you really get to enjoy the personality and daily milestones of the little person you are raising. The first crawls, steps, words, and kisses all hold a special place in the heart which can never be taken away. The process through which a baby learns language and communication is perhaps the most fascinating because they basically watch and observe everything that you do, and assign a meaning to it, then eventually learn how to say the word which represents it.

In your child, you see the potential for a much better version of yourself, as you vow not to let him or her make the same mistakes that you have. It's like watching the purest soul with unlimited potential learn about life and love every minute of the process. In many ways, I'm alive again and have renewed hope in life because of my son. The fast-paced nature of modern life slows down with a child because you get to enjoy the simple things in life again. Bubbles, puddles, sunshine, dirt, bugs, and worms are of vital importance to my son. I get to walk around smelling flowers again and catching lightning bugs.

These things used to be of vital importance to me too, but instead, bills and deadlines and trivial tasks have replaced them. With a child, the parent gets a return to their childhood—a carefree and happy time with unlimited possibility. Observing and enjoying the simple things in life again and taking the time to smell the roses and enjoy the journey allows you to see just how spectacular the human experience really is, and it fills you with hope of a brighter future. Never take for granted one day that you have with your baby, because you can't ever get that day back and you might miss something spectacular.

As your child grows, inevitably the teenage years approach, but before making judgments about your teenager, remember how difficult these times were for you too. Be there to give advice and avoid the costly mistakes that you made, but don't force opinions. Always be there to lend a hand and provide an open ear. Part of growing up is making mistakes, but raising your child to always make moral and ethical decisions from age two and on will help ensure that uncorrectable mistakes are avoided.

Just like childhood lets a parent slow down a bit, teenagehood lets a parent learn and relive their own memorable days. You get to watch your future superstar go to dances, compete in athletic events, and have fiery romances start and stop immediately. You get to experience again your own formative years while at the same time being super proud of your young man or woman. In addition, your teenager will also give you quite an education about the modern world, so in many ways, the parent becomes the student.

The innocence of youth is a real thing, and anyone who doesn't understand this concept does not deserve to be a parent and will certainly have to face this ugly demon upon life's completion. Being a parent is a privilege, not a rite. Not everyone can be a parent, so those blessed with this gift must cherish it. I consider anyone who abuses a child, or actually any living creature, the lowest form of humanity because, not only are you inflicting harm, you are robbing the individual of future happiness. If for some reason being a parent is not an option, don't do a half-assed or half-hearted job. Allow your child to be taken care of by someone who can give their whole heart and soul to the little person and is ready to accept this precious gift from God.

Unfortunately, some people who are ready and desperately want to be parents can't have a child of their own. However, not having a human child doesn't mean that you can't be a parent. I can say this confidently as someone who has raised many different varieties of pets and a baby: a pet will rely on you in much the same way as a baby does. You will experience first steps, first sounds, kisses, tail wags, and many other unique actions. They will develop a personality of their own, and you can enjoy the simple things in life with your pet. You will learn together and grow together. Being a good parent to a pet is just as important as being a good parent to a baby. All life is precious, and being a parent is a privilege, not a rite.

CHAPTER NINE

Where Does Intelligence Come From?

Every organism on earth has DNA or at least some form of genetic material which codes for how they develop into a mature organism and live life in general. The fossil record and theory of evolution state that from the primordial soup from which life emerged, genetic mutations allowed for formation of different species, and the species with the best adaptations survived and passed on their genes. We all have a common ancestor, which explains why, as an embryo, all species resemble a fish initially and then develop into the organism they are to become. Living creatures also have a tremendous amount of DNA in common with each other, such as a chimpanzee and a human having 98 percent in common or a human and zebra fish having 85 percent in common with each other, further supporting the fact of a common ancestor (genetics.thetech.org). It is in the sequences and segments of the DNA strand being activated that accounts for the great diversity of life.

If we all have a common ancestor and much of our DNA strand in common with all life on earth, then why are humans the only species to develop technology, think abstractly, and build such magnificent structures? Humans are able to develop technology, think abstractly, and construct incredible buildings because they don't have to worry as much as other species about survival and passing on genes to the next generation. If we think objectively about human beings, we could come to the conclusion that we as a species aren't the best at anything besides thinking, and even this can't be stated with 100 percent certainty because we can't get into the consciousness of other living organisms, so we don't exactly know what goes into their decision-making process.

Humans are not the fastest runners or swimmers. A cheetah can run much faster, and a tuna can swim much faster. Humans are not the best hunters. We need weapons and tools to hunt. Humans are not the best climbers or highest jumpers. Monkeys can climb much better, and white-tailed deer can clear an eight-foot fence. Humans don't possess the keenest of senses. A hawk can see much farther, a bat has sonar for hearing, and dogs can smell thousands of times better than humans. Humans are also not the best suited to their environment. We can't fly, live underwater, or survive in extremes without the help of special garments.

In many ways, human beings need technology and buildings in order to survive. If we hadn't as a species developed this ability to think and construct structures to hide in or build tools to hunt with and defend ourselves, other animals would have caught and killed us. It is because of our ability to think that we don't have to worry about survival as much as other species, and this allows us to use our minds for higher forms of thinking. However, not every individual in the human race is required to know how to develop technology and build a house. The point to this statement is that if an individual doesn't need this knowledge, then they won't exert energy trying to accomplish these tasks.

In the animal world, animals don't need to know how to develop technology, think abstractly, or build houses because they are so well suited to their environment. If they can outrun, outjump, outswim, or outsmart the predator trying to eat them, then they don't need a technology to help them survive. Animals only need to worry about surviving and passing on their genes to the next generation and never require the need for higher-order thinking. The danger comes with the superiority complex that humans seem to have over animals because of their ability for higher-order thinking.

We cannot enter the consciousness of other living species. We do not know what goes into an animal's decision-making process or even thought process. We assume to know and basically call an animal's ability to survive an instinct. In essence, an instinct is a preprogrammed way of behaving in order to survive. However, what if we replace the word *instinct* with *intelligence*? What if there is a myriad of environmental factors which an animal has to detect, interpret, and consider before doing anything? If we consider the sport of fishing and the phrase *the fish outsmarted us today*, this bizarre notion might seem logical.

Anyone who has ever gone fishing knows that you don't catch a fish on every single cast and that fish aren't located in every part of a lake or stream. Fish move around their environment to various locations, depths, and temperature gradients, and the weather, time of year, and time of day all play a part in determining their location. Expert anglers and professional fisherman recognize these patterns after years of experience and trial and error, but even they don't catch a fish on every cast or in every section of a lake. Sometimes a piece of information eludes the most skilled anglers and prevents them from finding fish. This means that the fish are using all of the information in their environment to make a decision about where to go in order to avoid getting caught or eaten.

Whether the decision is a conscious evaluation of environmental information or a preprogrammed response to external stimuli, no one can know for sure without entering the consciousness of the fish. However, preprogrammed responses to stimuli should be consistent over time, which would make them predictable over time. If we can predict where fish are and modern fish finders can even find fish using sonar, then why don't we catch fish on every attempt? The answer may be that fish are actually thinking and consciously evaluating information, which means that instinct is actually intelligence.

Modern technology will help us realize that humans aren't the only thinking and intelligent life forms on earth. Killer whales and bottle-nosed dolphins have a language involving various clicks and whistles, indicating that their brains can detect an environmental stimulus, interpret it, then send out a message in response, indicating intelligence. Some species of monkeys, such as the wild chimpanzee, can actually use tools to obtain food. They use a stick to dig out bugs from a hole in a tree. This indicates that the chimpanzee used some form of rationalization to devise a way to eat, indicating intelligence.

Animals can also detect and interpret human emotion. Recent MRI studies with dogs show that different parts of their brain become activated with emotions from their owner. Dogs can sense sadness, joy, anger, fear, sickness, and many other emotions. They react to various tones of voice and actually show emotion themselves. A tail between the legs indicates fear, while a wag of the tail indicates happiness. In order to show emotion, an animal must be able to understand their environment, indicating intelligence. Anyone who has a dog can verify this, but modern science is just beginning to support this with actual hard data.

Actually, as many pet owners will tell you, the more that you watch your pet interact with their environment, the better you can understand the complexities of their behavior and the intelligence that they actually display. For instance, both cats and dogs will thoroughly investigate any new item added to their home environment. They will sniff the item, look at the item, touch the item, and then determine if it is something to be feared or enjoyed. The ability to evaluate a new item in an environment and determine whether it is safe or not indicates intelligence.

The problem with determining and interpreting animal intelligence is that we don't think exactly like animals. The old adage to not make a judgment on someone until you have walked a mile in their shoes applies here. We don't know exactly how the human brain works yet, so we can't be expected to know how another animal's brain works. We can't have the same consciousness as another human being or even interpret the world exactly the same as another human; therefore, we can't know what it is like to be conscious as another animal.

If science can find the universal code for what it means to be conscious and to think, then we can know how animals think. If science can ever decipher what the various sounds that an animal makes mean, then we might find that the seemingly random noises made are actually a language. Until this happens, we will not know how intelligent any animal actually is. However, since we all come from a common ancestor, we can't assume that we are the only ones who can think or possess intelligence. Keen observation of the animal kingdom, advances in technology to determine the basis for consciousness and thought, and simple logic will help humans eventually understand that animals deserve respect because there is more going on in their heads then we know or can currently prove.

An interesting situation arises when we think about the animals which we use for food being thinking and conscious. However, it doesn't change the fact that we need them to survive, and every animal in nature must eat something which was once alive in order to survive. When we observe nature, we realize that although death is a part of life, nothing gets wasted. Animals respect their environment by not abusing it or taking more than they need. This is the important rule that humans must follow—respect for resources and not wasting. If we apply this to food animals, this means treating them humanely, affording them a healthy life while on earth, and not wasting their body, which is needed for our survival. No animal in nature ever wants to die or be eaten, but in order for others to survive, this must happen. Since this fact cannot change, we must respect and treat humanely those which we rely on for our survival.

CHAPTER TEN

Time Travel

Life is difficult sometimes. It isn't always easy to do the right thing or behave the proper way, and sometimes it might be nice to just go back in time and do it again. Sadly, this is not possible and never will be. We can't go back in time to change our past or go into the future to alter our present.

Scientists and physicists will argue that time travel will eventually be possible due to the theory that the time-space continuum can be bent with the formation of wormholes. A wormhole is a way of bending space on itself so that travel through space would not be linear. If you move your finger over a plain sheet of paper from one end to the next, it will take around two seconds to go that distance. However, if you fold the paper in half, your finger can reach the other end in much less time. This is what a wormhole though space is. Space travelers could travel great distances through space in relatively short amounts of time.

In addition, it is known that if you put an atomic clock in space and another one on Earth, the effects of gravity, or lack thereof, in space slows the atomic clock down, so more time passes on Earth than in space. In this regard, if we sent astronauts to another galaxy which was light-years away, they would age less than the people on Earth and basically would travel through time. When they returned to Earth, they would essentially be from the future relative to the people on Earth. I believe that this type of time travel will eventually be possible, but this really isn't the type of time travel that would allow us to change our past or future.

The reason that we can never go back in time to our past or ahead in time to our future has to do with the fact that we exist right now. Everything that we have done in the past has made us what we are today. If you go back in time to change an element from the past, it would alter your present state. Therefore, the element which was changed from the past would alter the entire sequence of events which made you the person you are right now. This means that in the present state you would not be the same person who originally needed the change. For example, let's say that right now you have a scar on your face which you wish wasn't there. If you went back in time to stop the event which led to the scar, you would alter the learning experience gained from sustaining an injury. This would make you either a slightly more cautious person or a slightly more daring person. A more daring person would conduct their life differently than a cautious person in the events following the avoided injury, which would lead to altered social relationships and altered life experiences, making you a different person than you were when you went back in time originally.

The same holds true for the future. Changing an element from the future would alter the entire sequence of events leading up to that future, making you a different person than you are right now. This is not an easy concept to deal with, but if we consider the butterfly effect, it makes sense. The butterfly effect is basically a theory that everything is interconnected in some capacity. So if a butterfly in Africa flaps its wings, the minute change in wind velocity can slightly alter an environmental factor in that habitat, leading to changes in other local habitats, and through a snowball effect, it might end up raining in America. The interconnections are immense, but basically everything in existence affects something else in some capacity.

Although we can't travel into our past or future to change our present, life does offer an alternative in some cases—the second chance. Second chances in life are not guaranteed, but if they present themselves, they offer a way to change our present state. We all have regrets or wishes that we could have done something differently in our past. Sometimes we can create a second chance, and other times we can't. Although we might have to live the rest of our lives with the bad feelings of a blown opportunity, the hope of an eventual redemption or the joy of fixing a mistake can make us better, more vigilant people. In my experience, getting a second chance and seizing the moment is one of the best feelings in life. You can feel good about yourself for correcting your own world. Take my word for it; you feel great about yourself for fixing the injustice which distorts the balance in both your life and other's lives.

My personal life can be described as a compilation of second chances. As a child, I was born with a heart problem called an atrial septal defect, which required surgery. My parents had the surgery done and gave me my first second chance in life. Later in life, as a teenage boy scout, I was trying to earn a merit badge called rabbit raising. My friend and I got some rabbits and tried to raise them and get them to breed. We really didn't have much experience with rabbits, and when one died, we had to give the other one back so that he was safe. I felt bad about this undertaking well into my thirties, as these rabbits should have been given a better life, and when I got the opportunity to adopt two rabbits from an animal shelter, I seized the moment. These rabbits now have their own room in my house with air conditioning and have a spectacular life. On a similar note, I also adopted a dog from the shelter (who now sleeps in my bed) and a kitten from the street (who sleeps on my couch), giving these pets a second chance at life.

As I entered my twenties, I made great number of mistakes. My roaring twenties was the decade when I was basically an alcoholic asshole. I was only concerned about myself and having a good time. I pushed away family and gave my parents many more gray hairs than they wanted for all of the times that I came home drunk or passed out somewhere and didn't let them know that I wasn't coming home. One particular instance stands out, and it was when I took my mom to Las Vegas for her birthday. To make a long story short, I basically ruined her trip by being a drunken mess. I said some things that I regretted and destroyed an opportunity to have a great time in a city that I love with a person that I love.

It took four years for me to correct this wrong, and it was because of my wife that I got the opportunity. My wife (live-in girl-friend at the time) almost left me because of the drinking. My family had an intervention, and I stopped with the alcohol. She was talked into staying with me by my family, and agreed to give me a second chance. Thank God that she did because she is the love of my life and I don't know what I would do without her. Life greatly improved after that, and we ended up getting married in Las Vegas. My parents also came out for the occasion, and we had a spectacular, sober wedding weekend. I got the opportunity to make up for a bad birthday trip with my mom, and my wife got the wedding of her dreams for giving me that second chance.

Sometimes, it takes a death for a second chance. When my grandfather—I called him Buddy—died, I put a note in his casket saying that I would step up and be a better man. I truly meant everything I said in the note, but the alcoholism of my twenties kept me being an asshole. When I stopped drinking, I became that better man, and life with all members of my family improved. It was when my grandmother died that I was able to put another note to my grandfather in her casket saying that I finally lived up to that promise. I also included a picture of my son, born two days before my nana died, so that she could show everybody in heaven.

These examples show that it may take years but second chances do come. I am still making up for wrongs that I committed in my early years, but I am trying to make things right. I encourage everyone to seize the moments when they come. Even if it is something small, like helping a person carry something to their car or picking up an item that an elderly person dropped so that they don't have to bend down, take my word for it, you will feel good about yourself, and you won't have to regret missing your opportunity. Regret is one of the worst feelings in life, but second chances are one of the best!

Occasionally, a celebrity or famous sports figure gets a second chance to publicly fix a blown opportunity or seize the moment. This past summer, LeBron James got his chance to fix something he didn't feel right about. LeBron James, for those of you who don't know, is the world's best basketball player. He was born and raised in northern Ohio and got drafted into the NBA right out of high school to the Cleveland Cavaliers. LeBron was a superstar in Cleveland, and the people loved him, but he just couldn't win an NBA title there. Therefore, after seven years, he decided to leave Cleveland and play for the Miami Heat. He let the people know that he was leaving Cleveland through a primetime TV special, and to say the least, the people of northern Ohio were devastated. Some people even burned his jersey.

LeBron was a superstar in Miami, though, and won two NBA championships and was a great figure for charities in the community. However, when he had the opportunity to opt out of his contract and become a free agent, he seized the moment. Many other NBA teams courted him to try to recruit his talents to their NBA team, but LeBron's heart never left Cleveland. After weeks of speculation, he let everyone know through a very well-written and heartfelt essay that he was returning to Cleveland to win the city a title that it has been seeking for decades. LeBron needed to leave Cleveland to learn how to become a champion, but he never really felt home in Miami. His initial decision to leave Cleveland also never quite felt right, so he seized the moment when it presented itself.

His return to Cleveland, called the Return of the King, reenergized the entire city and fan base. The people of Cleveland got their hometown son back, and season tickets sold out within hours. It is projected to also boost many of Cleveland's downtown businesses, which suffered when he left town. A city which has seen its share of bad times has hope again because of one man's actions. Many of us will never get an opportunity quite like this, but even the little things that we do in life to fix the problems we create can make a huge difference in our own little world. Seizing the moment, like LeBron James did, can wipe away regret and inspire hope in all of our lives.

CHAPTER ELEVEN

Holidays Are Important but Not Essential

There are days throughout the year which commemorate certain important events or people and basically force individuals to stop and think about the magnitude of said day for a moment. Christmas, Easter, Mother's Day, Father's Day, Fourth of July, Memorial Day, and Valentine's Day are just a few examples of when people get together and focus on something important. The problem arises when an individual only focuses on the special person or event for that day because it diminishes the fact that they are important every day of the year. For example, on Mother's Day we all try to make Mom feel special and honor her for the day. However, isn't it more important to honor Mom every day of the year since she was the one who gave birth to you and without her you wouldn't exist? Soldiers died for our freedom, so should we only think about them on Memorial Day? Jesus overcame evil and rose from the dead on Easter; isn't this message important every day? The point is that holidays force us to think about an event for the day, but these events are so important that we need to think about them daily. When we honor our mother or father daily, respect our vets daily, and pray to Jesus daily, we can eliminate the pressure which we sometimes feel to get everything right on one particular day.

The details of a holiday are not important; the gathering of family and friends for the true essence of the holiday is. It is unfortunate that families cannot all come together as regularly as they like. Whether it is the hustle and bustle of daily life or the fact that sometimes family members just don't get along well, oftentimes for a holiday they can put aside their differences and find time. Holidays almost become the reason for families to gather, and the true meaning of the holiday sometimes gets lost in the minute details which accompany bringing families together.

For example, I often get in wars during the holidays with my wife over the house needing to be immaculately clean in order for any guests to come over. The condition of the house is consistent for 364 days of the year, but for the one day that people come over, we have to be fake and pretend that we live in a spotless palace, and I don't believe in being fake under any circumstance. The appearance of the house becomes more important than the message of the holiday, and the fight that ensues makes everyone involved not in the mood to entertain. The result is that the holiday gets ruined, and the anticipation of future holiday gatherings causes so much anxiety that it leads to cancellations.

Another more widespread example of details destroying a day is on Christmas when the gift becomes more important than the act of giving. Retail establishments bombard people during Christmas with gift propaganda, and eventually consumers get brainwashed into thinking that the gift is the only important part of Christmas. Santa Claus, who was originally intended to be an example of charity and gift giving to those in need, has become simply a bringer of toys for kids—a delivery man whose true essence has been destroyed by stores and malls. It has become sad, and this past year, while saying grace on Christmas Eve, I delivered this prayer to my family to help get the message across:

"Santa Claus is real.

"A long time ago, about 1,700 years to be precise, St. Nicholas started, or rather famously continued, a great tradition: he gave something that he had to someone in need. Back in those times, the parents of a young girl had to pay a dowry to her potential husband in order to take her. A man with three daughters at the time didn't have the money to pay three dowries, and in order to avoid the girls being forced into prostitution, St. Nicholas tossed a bag of gold pieces down the man's chimney to avoid such a fate. From that kind act, the legend of Santa Claus began.

"Adults may feel that the story of Santa Claus is only for kids due to such things as the village at the North Pole, flying sleighs and reindeer, and an old, fat man who delivers presents to every good boy and girl on earth. However, if we consider that these things are just embellishments to put a face and story on the true message of Christmas, we see that the spirit of Santa Claus is real. There are many things that we believe in but can't see, for example, Wi-Fi, love, and evil. We assign a Wi-Fi symbol to visualize it. We picture love as hearts floating around to conceptualize it. We say the devil is responsible for all evil to give a face to horrific acts. We all know that these things exist despite not being able to see them,

but we need a concrete objects assigned to them to make them more acceptable. Therefore, we assign the spirit of giving, generosity, and helping others to Santa Claus.

"So is the concept of a man being generous to someone in need only for kids? I think not. The act of St. Nicholas lives on, no matter where you live or how old you are. Maybe your present isn't wrapped up under a tree but rather a feeling you get by being around loved ones or a secret wish that comes true.

"Santa Claus delivers all of these things to everyone on earth who believes in being generous and helping others.

"So I ask again, is it really Santa Claus that you don't believe in or just the wrapping?

"Merry Christmas!"

I will not deny it; holidays have become very difficult for me. For my son's sake, I put on a happy face and do the best that I can to make it a wonderful day for him and forge happy memories of the day, but inside, I'm in turmoil. This forced me to sit down and think about what a holiday really is, and I have determined that every day should be thought of as a holiday. The special event for which the holiday was made is important every day of the year, so thank your mom and dad daily, pray to the Lord for the life you have, praise a veteran for their service, and enjoy the people around you.

A formal gathering isn't required to get the family together; sometimes the impromptu meetings make the greatest memories. Give a gift when you feel like giving a gift; charity is a virtue that can be served daily. Being generous doesn't need to occur on only certain days. When you allow yourself to think in this manner, a holiday remains important but not essential, because you live a holiday daily. In addition, the minor details which become so burdensome during a holiday get minimized because all of your attention isn't focused on one day and you can actually enjoy the day.

CHAPTER TWELVE

Pontius Pilate Was a Coward

In Christianity, Jesus is considered God the Son, one-third of the Holy Trinity. The other two-thirds of the Holy Trinity are God the Father and God the Holy Spirit. Whether or not a person believes in the trinity doesn't dispute the fact that Jesus was a man that lived on earth nearly two thousand years ago. Being a Christian, I have been taught about Jesus for my entire life. After breaking down all of the stories I have heard about Jesus, I have come to the conclusion that Jesus was an incredible man who loved others with His whole heart and practiced what He preached, even until the moment He died. He performed miracles on the sick, fed the hungry, and spoke to all who would listen about how to get along with and love one another. It was Jesus who said, "The greatest gift you can ever give is to lay down your life for a friend." Whether or not Jesus was divine or the Son of God isn't as important as His message and actions, which I believe make Him a God to be worshipped, praised, followed, and revered as perhaps the greatest human being to ever live. The way He led His life is the way we need to live our life.

Despite all of the great things that Jesus did in life, there was a group of people that didn't like what He was saying or doing because it wasn't the religion they were used to practicing. On His final day, Jesus was brought before a Roman judge by a crowd hoping to have Him executed for blasphemy. After talking with Jesus, the Roman judge, Pontius Pilate, found that Jesus wasn't guilty of any crimes and was just perhaps a dreamer. Pontius Pilate had Jesus whipped and beaten severely to teach Him a lesson and then planned on releasing Him. However, the crowd wanted Jesus crucified, and fearing the mob would riot, Pilate said that he washed his hands of this man's blood and had Jesus crucified. Jesus readily accepted His death on the cross to prove the point that He truly loved everyone, even those who persecuted and tortured Him. Jesus proved that death and sin would not win over justice and compassion, and in doing so, allowed the rest of humanity to be saved if they believed in Him.

What if Pilate had the courage to do what he believed was right? Why was he a coward and did give in to a crowd wanting an innocent man killed? His soldiers were present and could easily have controlled the crowd. It is said that Pilate did what he did to not cause trouble for his superiors and maintain his job. An innocent man died a horrible death so that one man could keep his job. In my opinion, Pontius Pilate may be the one of the lowest and most disgraceful examples of a human being. Self-preservation was more important than justice and doing what's right. If Pilate stood up for what he knew was right that day, Jesus would have been able to continue His sacred mission, and the crowd and all those present would have seen that justice and compassion was more important than maintaining the status quo and self-preservation. I don't know how the world might have changed that day, but at least one man could have been proud that he stood up to adversity and did the right thing.

Sadly, this disregard for doing what is right in the face of adversity continues to happen in today's society. We are a selfish society whose main concern is, number one, ourselves. This needs to change. For every action, there is a reaction somewhere else. Everything that we do in life is not isolated in a vacuum. We must be responsible for our actions. Cheating to get ahead will only reveal your shortcomings later in life. Omitting information to save face, a job, or even a relationship may temporarily work, but the truth always comes out. When you intentionally hurt another person or animal, your evil deeds will later haunt your memories and thoughts. For all of our actions in this life, I believe that we will have to answer for them before passing to the next life. Even if you don't believe in that, is it worth taking the chance? Doing the right thing in life is not always the easiest, cheapest, or most popular choice, but it is by far the easiest to live with.

CHAPTER THIRTEEN

Humanity Is Not Ready to Learn Our True Identity

People as a whole are stupid. People as individuals are highly intelligent. When people get together in groups, it is much easier to just go with the flow and maintain status quo rather than go against the current and stand up for what is right. As examples, I give you Jesus Christ and Dr. Martin Luther King Jr. Jesus went to His death teaching people that the most important commandment is to love one another and that His way is the path to heaven, a stance which went against the very rigid laws of the day involving religion, sacrifices to God the Father, and helping and curing the sick and sinners. Dr. King wanted to put an end to segregation in America through inspiring speeches and nonviolent protests and paid his life in the process. Separate but equal was the trend in America at the time, but Dr. King saw that this really only meant separate and not equal, so he taught that all people are equal and separation wasn't necessary. In both of these cases, any reasonable individual can see the genius and truth in what these men taught and believed, but going against the norm and the way things were done at the time meant isolation, persecution, and scrutiny from the community. Therefore, life is just easier if you go with the flow.

In today's society, everything that anyone does is open to scrutiny from everyone thanks to social media. If someone posts information or a picture on social media, rest assured that someone will have a comment about it. One of the problems lies in the fact that all relevant information is often not included or available with a post or tweet or Instagram, and opinions start to form, groups amass, and public opinion grows based on an incomplete piece of information. As I said before, whether these opinions are right or wrong, it is just easier to follow the lead and not go against public opinion. However, someone will always go against public opinion, and they become vulnerable to the wrath of the masses in the popular opinion group, and conflict, in some way, is commenced.

The select groups of individuals chosen to lead the people of earth can see that society is just not ready for the truth about the world or man's place in it. Conspiracy theories exist about governments withholding information from the public, and there are probably secret societies throughout the world with secret knowledge about alien life and the origin of man or maybe even highly confidential religious information. Looking at the current state of the world and the fact that we have wars, racism, a go-with-the-flow attitude, and social media, which opens everything up to public opinion, can any reasonable and logical person really say that we are ready for higher knowledge about our existence? The answer is a resounding "absolutely not."

Anyone watching the history of this planet from afar will see that human beings clearly can't get along with one another, so introducing a newer, more intelligent alien life would be disastrous. The people in the government can also recognize this, which is why no United States president has ever released any information about extraterrestrial life. I also speculate that the secret societies, such as the Free Masons, keep their information secretive and have members prove their worthiness of this information over years because they too know that people in general just aren't ready yet. When we change as a whole human race, the information will become available, and perhaps anyone watching from afar might make their presence known when they see a more accepting humanity. Until that day when people can accept all members of their own species (which makes racism seem even more asinine), we won't meet a new species.

Twenty-Five Thoughts

1. All that we are guaranteed in life is the moment that we are in right now. Life might end at any time. Make each moment count, as it very well might be your last. Try to never go to bed mad; you may not wake up in the morning. Let your loved ones know that you love them, just in case you don't get the chance later.

2. Everything that we do in life will be judged. It will be judged by people in this life and by our Creator after this life is over. Keep this in mind with every action you make, as every choice that you make in life will eventually catch up with you. For those people in the spotlight—such as professional athletes, actors, actresses, and political figures—remember that kids look up to you and adults want to be like you. Don't throw away something that you worked so hard to achieve by lapses in judgment. Use your platform to set a good example.

3. Friends will come and go throughout life. Your best friends in school might be mere acquaintances later in life. A true friend takes years to find but will never leave your side, regardless of how they feel about what you are doing. A true friend can be anyone, even a pet or a family member. You can only be a friend or have a friend when you truly love the other person.

4. Live life in black and white and avoid the gray areas. Think of everything as right or wrong, or good and evil. When you simplify life into this dichotomy and eliminate the uncertainty, choices become easier to make, and the direction of your life

becomes clear. If you live in a gray area, doubt will always exist, which leads to regret.

5. Regret is one of the worst feelings in life. When and if you get a second chance, seize it! The terrible feelings of wishing that something was different become replaced by the feeling that something wrong was made right.

6. Be proud of the person that you are. Take pride in yourself and your accomplishments, but keep it to yourself. Bragging makes you seem like an asshole and opens you up to criticism from others, which deflates your self-esteem. When you stay humble yet internally proud, a compliment that you receive raises your self-esteem even higher.

7. Don't half-ass anything. When you decide to do something, go after it with your whole heart and leave nothing behind. Whatever you do in life, fully commit to it. Even if you fail, you can say that you tried your best and had nothing left to give. Not trying your best will lead to regret later in life, and sometimes, you can't get that second chance. Imagine if a surgeon only tried 75 percent as hard as he could during a procedure. Would that benefit anyone? Give 100 percent all of the time.

8. In every competition in life, there is a winner and a loser. Teaching children that everyone is a winner is not accurate. Being the loser makes you try harder to be the winner. Take Michael Jordan as an example; he had to lose numerous times and push himself to places he didn't think he could go, in order to win. As a result, he molded himself into a champion and perhaps the finest basketball player and competitor the world has ever known. Losing isn't fun, but when you try your best, it can be accepted and turned into motivation.

9. Enjoy the little things in life. Take time to smell the roses and experience the sights and sounds of life. There may not be a later time for you to do this. It is important to enjoy the path as much as the final destination.

10. Honor your commitments. If you can't live up to your promise, either don't make the commitment or try harder to fulfill it. In

regard to marriage or relationships, don't enter into one if you can't remain faithful and true to the other person. In regard to professional athletes and professional sports owners, this means honoring the signed contract. If you can't honor a long-term agreement, then sign a short contract and renegotiate more often. When an athlete holds out from performing under his current contract because he or she wants more money, it makes the athlete seem like a greedy asshole, and resentment will eventually follow from the majority of fans who dream of making even a tenth of what an athlete makes.

11. For all of the athletes out there, never argue with the referee about a call that is made. With the exception of instant replays and coaches' challenges, have you ever seen a referee change his or her call on the field after a player argues about it? The answer is no. When a player argues with a referee, it makes the player seem like a pompous ass because it implies that the referee, who witnessed the play, can't judge it as accurately as the person who didn't witness the play, and therefore indicates that the referee is stupid in comparison. If anything, the referee will be more inclined to judge the next play even harder and not in favor of the player arguing about the call. In addition, the time spent complaining will oftentimes put the player in a bad position for the next play, which will be detrimental to the team. Also, have you ever seen a referee go up to a player and say, "Wow, that was a dumb play you just made"? This is the equivalent of when a player argues with a referee about a call. The answer is no, and the reason is because that would be disrespectful to the player. Therefore, show respect for the game and the referee by not complaining about calls, because it won't change the outcome of the call and will only hurt the team.

12. Pay school teachers more money. School teachers are the ones responsible for molding the individuals which will run our future societies. They both babysit and educate our future eight hours per day, 5 days per week, 180 days per year. Teachers have perhaps the most responsibility of any job next to physicians and health care workers. Let's pay them what they deserve.

13. Support and honor our soldiers. Even if the war or conflict has questionable motives, it is these brave men and women who do the job which I personally know I am not brave enough to do. These individuals follow the orders of their superiors, risking life and limb, to accomplish a goal, and often pay the price for years to come afterward. Afford these brave souls the honor, respect, and resources that they need as payment for the job which we don't have the balls to do ourselves.

14. As a whole, the human race needs to smarten up. As long as racism, wars, terrorism, and other atrocities continue occurring, we will never get the truth about the universe and our place in it. As I said before, if we can't get along with one another, then how are we going to get along with a more advanced and intelligent alien, or extraterrestrial, race? The abundance of knowledge that we can gain would far outweigh any resolution or result from war or conflict. If we can learn to accept other individuals in our own species first, then we could begin to accept other civilizations from other worlds. Until that day, we will continue to be a warring and relatively violent society with no idea of our place in the universe.

15. Ask the question "should we?" rather than "could we?" Scientific advancements are occurring at an incredible rate, but just because we can do something doesn't mean that it's a good idea. For example, genetic manipulation may one day cure diseases and extend life many years, but if life in those extra years is poor in quality, such that individuals can't eat or move on their own, is it worth living those extra years? I'm suggesting that we contemplate all possible outcomes of scientific advancements before we blaze forward with them.

16. Respect life. We cannot create life on our own, so we must accept the fact that someone greater than us has given humans, animals, and the world around us this incredible gift. Even in the making of a baby, two cells may come together, but an extra element is needed to give the combo the spark of life. It is perfectly acceptable to use the world and its resources to survive, but we must respect the planet and realize that other living

organisms have just as much right to live on the planet as we do, and the fact that someone thought highly enough of other species to give them the incredible gift too proves this.

17. Wear what you feel comfortable in. Fashion that looked stupid twenty years ago still looks stupid today, and fashion that looks stupid today will still look stupid in twenty years. Why waste mental energy wondering what other people think about what you are wearing? Wear what makes you feel good.

18. Let the hatred, resentment, and grudges go. I am very guilty of holding grudges, and some things I have yet to reconcile in my mind, but I am trying. As the pastor of Mary, Mother of God parish Cyril Edwards said, "Hatred and grudges live rent-free in your mind. Let them go and use that space for better things." This is certainly true, as a great deal of mental energy is used in holding on to hatred and resentment. When and if you can let them go, the mental energy saved allows you to think clearer.

19. Today is a great day to start something new. Why wait until tomorrow? Tomorrow may not come. Start the new diet, new exercise program, new way of thinking, new project today and feel good at night that you took the first step toward something better. Do away with New Year's resolutions; start them today!

20. Listen to the people who have already walked down your path. Advice about life is invaluable. I was an alcoholic for about ten years, and I wouldn't listen to anybody, even former alcoholics, about the consequences and prices that you'll pay. As I found out the hard way, they were right about everything. The first people to walk down a path make mistakes and learn from them. It doesn't make much sense to try it yourself and make the same mistakes. Ask for help when help is available; however, don't offer advice until someone asks, because it only falls on deaf ears. When someone is ready for help and ready to listen, they will ask.

21. Reuse and recycle. It gives our planet, from which we've taken so much, a second chance.

22. Get the help you need before it's too late. Worrying about what could be wrong or suffering through what is wrong puts

so much stress on the body that it makes whatever is wrong worse. There is always help out there; no problem is unfixable. Sometimes there is no cure, but there are ways to ease the pain.

23. Stand up to bullies. A bully will abuse anyone he or she deems weaker as a mask for their own shortcomings and insecurities. Be proud of who you are and stand up for yourself. As you go through life, people will try to take advantage of you and walk all over you, but when you put a stop to this behavior, you will both boost your own self-esteem for being confident in yourself and make the bully fix their own deficiencies.

24. Use the talents that your Creator blessed you with. Whether it helps one life or many, the gifts bestowed on you are intended to be used. Talents can be anything from athletic ability to entertaining to even providing companionship and comfort. Although the purpose of all talents may not be clear at this time, not using them is like spitting in the face of the One that made you because it shows that your intentions and plan are more important. Everything in life has a purpose, and the talents we're given are the tools with which we fulfill that purpose.

25. Be open to new ideas and new ways of thinking. The impossible will eventually be possible, as hope can get you through many dark times, and imagination can lead you to brighter times. Sometimes it may not seem like anyone is watching or caring, but the Divine Creator knows everything about everyone to which he or she has given life, even if that seems impossible. Nicholas Cage said it best in the movie *City of Angels*: "Some things are true whether you believe them or not."

The End

Am I Proud of Today?

A Workbook for Life
developed by Jason Hapstak

Am I proud of today? What a loaded question with only two answers. Answering a few, or all, of these questions daily will help you to respond truthfully to this question. I encourage you to even write down your answers to these questions as it may help you to recognize patterns. Whatever you decide to do, the only directions to this exercise are to be honest and to respond either positively or negatively; neutrality is just a delay in the true answer.

The Morning

When you wake up in the morning, oftentimes the first thing you will hear is the alarm clock. When you hear it, are you excited to start the day off or pissed that you have to get up already? You had no guarantee when you went to bed the night before if you would wake up at all. In this regard, the alarm clock is a blessing. If you wake up annoyed, is that really the way you want to thank your Maker for allowing you to get up today?

The next activity on the list is often making yourself aware of what is going on around you. Did you ever just look around to see who else made it through the night? Maybe your wife or kids are next to you, or maybe your cat or dog sleeps by your side. Do you ever say thanks for this blessing? Maybe you sleep alone. Have you ever just listened to the birds sing in the morning for a few moments? Birds have an angelic and peaceful harmony; maybe take a few minutes to hear it. Have you ever just woken up and taken a deep breath? Did you ever notice how good that felt? I bet that if you woke up and couldn't breathe one day, you would miss the days when you could fill up those lungs. We can either take all of these things for granted, or we can just say thanks. Which do you think would better enable you to be proud of your overall day?

When preparing breakfast, do you complain about what you are having or the fact that you have to cook something? Many people in the world wake up to nothing to eat; I bet that would be a lot worse than not having the right type of cereal. Maybe you see someone for the first time at breakfast. Do you greet them with cheer and vigor or just acknowledge that they are alive? I bet the other person feels great when the latter happens. Do you give your dog or cat or other creature a nice pet in the morning? I guarantee that if they weren't there, you would have wished that you petted them more often.

After breakfast, a person usually prepares for work or the day's activities. Even if you hate your job, it's probably better than having no job at all. If the day's activities aren't on your list of favorite things to do, I bet that if you were bedridden or too sick to get out of bed, anything would be better than that. Before you leave for work, do you say good-bye to your spouse and kids, or do you run out of the door? Do you realize that when you say good-bye to someone, it may very well be the last time that you ever see them? This is a regret that many people have because everyone thinks that they have more time to do it later, but you aren't guaranteed that. Make it count while you have the opportunity.

On your way to work or the day's activities, do you ever acknowledge how nice it is to have a ride? I bet that if you had to walk, not voluntarily, any sort of vehicle or bus ride would be good. Do you ever take in the scenery on the way to work? I imagine that if everything got burned down or destroyed by something, the trees and bushes might seem nice in comparison. Sometimes there is traffic on the way to work. Is getting pissed or developing road rage going to miraculously eliminate the traffic? Some things in life are just annoying and unavoidable, but maybe you can make good use of your time by enjoying your morning coffee or listening to a nice song instead of flipping off the construction workers.

Once you arrive at work, do you dillydally and waste time, or do you give an honest effort? Even if you are the only one at work who actually works, at least you can be proud of yourself for giving a true attempt. To your coworkers, are you courteous or miserable? Look at it this way: if they all got laid off, someone would have to do their work too, probably you. I bet that would be less desirable than just saying hi and giving a nice smile at work. To your customers or patients, do you talk down to them or make it seem like they aren't important? How do you feel when that happens to you?

For doctors and health professionals especially, who have a wealth of knowledge about medicine, imagine if you visited a rocket scientist or theoretical physicist and they gave you a ten-word explanation in a five-minute visit about what they were doing. How stupid would you feel and pissed would you be? Now imagine how pissed off your patients are when you do the same. Every professional has knowledge about their field, and every patient usually has less knowledge about that field. It is your job to take the time, listen, and explain things in a way that is understandable.

For every occupation that deals with people, remember that without customers, you don't have a job. In addition, for customers, without employees, you don't have a service. When you make a checkout experience pleasant, it goes a long way to making everyone's day better. Both customers and employees alike may not remember every decent checkout or service experience, but they do remember every bad one. Being courteous and respectful in a checkout line will help you to be proud of your day. When you are on you cell phone checking out, do you think it's courteous to the teller? It shows that they aren't important enough to acknowledge them fully. I bet that if the teller was on their cell phone, it would not go over well. The bottom line is when you are at work, are you diligent and courteous or lackadaisical and rude? What would you be proud of?

The Evening

When work ends, the second part of your day begins. How do you feel about going to your children's sporting events? Are you mad that you have to be there, because you have so many other things to do, or are you excited to see them compete and try their best? Remember, when these days are over and your kids go off to college and aren't around very much, you will wish you had these days back. If you decided to go to their games, were you paying attention or sitting there aloof? Were you on social media checking posts or tweets or Instagrams?

Do yourself a favor. If you decide to go, go there and be engaged because this is the only way that you can be proud of yourself for this action. Social media may be nice to quickly catch up on news or current events, but other than that, it is relatively useless. It is the equivalent of gossip and tabloids. Who really cares what someone else thinks about a subject? Every moment that you spend looking down at your phone or tablet is a moment that you miss the beauty and splendor of the natural world around you. Is being current on all the new trends or posts something to be proud of?

Many people go shopping after work, which can be for either leisure or necessity. Have you ever complained about grocery shopping? Imagine if you had to hunt for your dinner or go into the forest to gather it, would that be easier? I bet grocery shopping wouldn't be so bad in this situation.

Do you exercise after work? Is it annoying or pleasurable? If you were paralyzed, you would long for the days when you could walk a treadmill for twenty minutes. Even if you have to trudge through exercise on a daily basis, remember this: you are maintaining and making stronger the greatest instrument that that God will ever give you.

Oftentimes people meet after work, and sometimes a person will wait all day for this opportunity. For instance, maybe an elderly relative waited till evening for you to come over and have a snack with them. Did you hurry them when you came over because you had other places to be, or did you enjoy your time with each other? How would you feel if you were rushed through something that you waited all day for?

Maybe you met some friends after work to have a few drinks. Were you responsible, and did you avoid driving intoxicated? If you did drive home, did you realize that you endangered everyone else on the road with the potential for death? Did you drink so much that you couldn't remember what happened? Is this anything to be proud of?

Maybe you had a meeting with your spouse after work. Did you carry all of the burdens of your day into this interaction? Were you in a bad mood for the duration? How do you think this makes the other person feel? When you are pleasant and sociable in an interaction, everyone walks away a winner.

Some people eat dinner with the family after work. Good mood or bad mood? Did you make everyone's dinnertime peaceful, or did you incite a fight? Did you ask anyone else about their day? Sometimes this allows other people to vent and feel better. Did you tell anyone about your day? When you keep it a secret, it sometimes makes other people feel like they are unworthy of your words.

Do you have household chores to do after work? I bet that if you didn't have a house, you would wish for one that you could take care of. Or better yet, how does sleeping in the woods or on the street sound?

What about walking the dog after work? Is that annoying too? I bet that your dog waits all day for this opportunity and feels amazing when he/she finally gets to go. Sometimes, taking notice of how happy doing an activity makes someone can actually make you happy too.

Did you enjoy any sort of nature after work, or did you run inside the house and sit on a couch? Did you feel any sun on your body today? Even if you have problems with the sun, you can wear sunscreen or clothes with coverage and feel the sun's warmth. Did you feel a breeze run through your hair? Even if it is winter, that crisp, cool air filling your lungs feels spectacular. Did you go by any running water today? Have you ever noticed how calming and peaceful the sound of a stream is? What about trees or beautiful colors of the foliage? Have you taken any notice of them today? If you feel that the inside of a house surpasses all of these things to the point that they don't need to be viewed or appreciated, then you have nothing to be ashamed of. However, one day you might become blind or lose your hearing; maybe then these simple things might be missed, even longed for.

Bedtime

Have you ever gazed at the stars at night? Have you ever noticed how beautiful the heavens are? Doing this can sometimes give you perspective on the fact that there is infinite potential out there. Just as every star helps to make the sky a little brighter, you have that potential as well. You can make this world a little better and add more brightness to it. Have you done that today?

Do you say good night to your family? There is a fifty-fifty chance that you might not see them ever again. If a disaster were to strike, what would you want your last words that night to have been?

Do you go to bed mad? I bet that would be a horrible last emotion to have had toward a person if you were to never see them again. In addition, what does it accomplish? Will the person that wronged you apologize to you in their sleep? Make no mistake about it; forgiveness is a subjective action. You cannot change the behaviors or actions of others, but you can control your emotional response to those actions. Staying mad drains out your mental energy because you are allowing something negative to live rent-free in your head.

Let it go. Forgiveness is for your own benefit, not the other person. In the future, perhaps you can make suggestions to a person about how their behavior affected you, and maybe they can change that behavior, but staying mad over an action which cannot be altered or changed accomplishes nothing but heartache and mental fatigue. The old proverb "forgive and forget" is the equivalent of pressing the reset or refresh button. Did you keep playing the same old game today where you lose in the end, or did you press the button to give yourself a chance at a new game with a better result possible?

Do you go to bed stressed out from the current day or the upcoming day? Whether you like it or not, you have one shot with every day to get it right and do your best. Stressing out about it at night will not change what has already occurred. All that you can hope for is another opportunity to try to get tomorrow right. And if tomorrow does come, there is nothing that you can do to try to stop it or slow it down, so there is no use in worrying about it. God has a destiny for all of us. We are not meant to know what the final chapter will be; however, if we do our best with the day we currently have, then at least we can say that we got the last part right.

Do you ever pray at night and thank God for your day? How do you feel when you do something nice for someone and they don't even acknowledge it? You aren't entitled to any blessings. God gave you them because He loves you. Even if you can't see it at the time because hard times have fallen upon you, every second that you are alive serves a purpose in the grand scheme of things. Be thankful for the opportunity even though life might not currently be going the way that you wish. Look at it this way: things can always be worse.

Did you give anyone a compliment today? It feels pretty nice to get a compliment. I bet that others would like it too.

Did you thank any military personnel today? They risk their lives for you so that you can live free. Thanks are always in order.

Did you commit any random acts of kindness today? If you are ever the recipient of this, it absolutely stuns you with joy and amazement! Try doing this for someone else and see how you feel. If a random act of kindness didn't happen today, how about just doing a kind act for someone you know? When people help each other and stop focusing on themselves, everyone can see, even for just a moment, that the world can be a better place if we try.

Did you do anything that you are ashamed of today? Did something occur where you just say to yourself, "Wow, I wish I didn't do or say that"? Once words leave your mouth or actions are committed, they can't be taken back. However, atonement can occur for these shameful acts. Did you learn from your mistakes today? Did you fix what was wrong? Did you apologize and vow not to let it happen again?

As sure as death and taxes, mistakes will occur, but it is what we do after the mistakes that matters. Second chances are one of the greatest gifts that God gives us, and if you happen to get one, seize it! A mistake can haunt you for decades, but when you erase the mistake by doing it right on the second attempt, the demons that haunt you are vanquished.

Did you intentionally or unintentionally hurt any feelings today? Damaging someone's self-esteem can be devastating, and if someone has preexisting issues with self-esteem, this exponentially adds to the problem. Analyze your whole day from multiple points of view before answering this question. It never feels good to get hurt, and a person's perception of a comment can differ greatly from the original intention. There is an old saying which goes, "If you can't say anything nice, then don't say anything at all." Basically, give compliments or keep quiet.

Did you smile today? Things can always be worse; be grateful that they aren't.

Did you stand up for yourself today, or did you let others step all over you? Did you hide your values because you were afraid of consequences? When you hide what you believe (not due to a life or death situation) due to fear of scorn from others, you accomplish nothing. The mental anguish that you will experience later will far outweigh what you gain from avoiding ridicule. Don't cower from a bully; step up to the bully, stand your ground, and knock him or her down if you have to. Even if you lose, you win on the inside, and that is where it matters most. A bully will always try to pick on the weak but will think twice about doing it again when a counterpunch will occur. How was your footing today?

Did you act ethically today? A business professor once told me, "Good ethics is good business." This is also true in life. A morally sound decision, even though you might lose or gain nothing from it, will ensure that your mind will be at peace.

Did you lose your temper today? Did it solve anything? Did it make the original situation better or worse?

Did you use your talents today? God gave everyone a special knack for doing something well. Not using a talent is like watching a flower wither and die. With special care, a plant will grow and flower. With use and practice, a talent will also grow into something spectacular. Did you water your plant today or allow it to be thirsty?

Did you give anyone bad news today? How did you act while delivering this information? How do you like to be presented with unpleasant details? Did you make the situation seem hopeless? Remember this: miracles do happen. I believe that miracles come from God or others who have passed from this life on to the next, but even if you have trouble accepting this, the mathematical laws of probability state that even if there is a one-in-one-trillion chance of something extraordinary happening, it has to happen at least once if it was tried a trillion times. The miracle isn't that something spectacular happens; it is that something spectacular happens to you.

There is no such thing as never or always in life. There is an exception to every rule, and even if a brilliant scientific mind tells you that there are universal laws which hold true throughout the universe in every situation, ask the scientist if he or she has been to every part of the universe during every possible scenario to prove that this theorem is correct. If every variable is not accounted for, then the best prediction is merely a guess. My point is when you get bad news or a bad prognosis or a probability of something happening, it is only a guess based on experience, limited variables, and observation of part of the whole situation. It is not a definitive declaration of your destiny.

Miracles happen, and they can happen to you. Therefore, in every situation, never eliminate hope because at the very least, if the tables were turned and the news giver became the news recipient, they would not want to be left hopeless. Did you crush any dreams today or leave the door open for hope?

Did you truly enjoy anything today? Did you savor the food you ate? Did you admire the beauty of a site you saw? Did you appreciate any music you heard today, either from nature or from man? Did you notice the softness of your clothes today? How about the warmth of your blankets or the comfort of your favorite chair? Did you relish any experiences that you had today? The little things in life are what you can control. Oftentimes, the big things are out of your control. You certainly would miss the little things in life if they were taken from you. It doesn't take much to appreciate what you have. Did you take anything for granted today?

Is there anything that I would like to change about today? This is a great place to start with the analysis of your day. In addition, if tomorrow comes, it's a great way to start your to-do list for that day. One of the great parts about life is that you don't have to wait long to get a fresh start. Every day offers a fresh opportunity to start something new. There is no use in waiting to start learning new subjects, exercising, eating differently, or trying something new. The only thing that waiting accomplishes is leading to regrets, and regrets are just unfulfilled hopes. If you want to fix a regret, you can start immediately. Seize the opportunity to make a wrong a right or fulfill a dream when it comes to you. You may never get a second chance, but if you do, attack it. Do you have any regrets today?

CONCLUSION

Every situation in life has two outcomes: it can go good or it can go poorly. Neutrality is not an option because being neutral is just a way of delaying an answer or commitment. You can be proud of the way that you act, or you can be disappointed with your actions. The three most important questions to ask yourself daily are these: Did I appreciate my world today? How did I treat other people today? Did I thank God today? If today is the final chapter in the story of your life, are you proud of today?

SPECIAL THANKS

I would like to thank God for giving me a shot at life. I would like to thank my parents for molding me into the man that I am today. I want to thank my wife for encouraging me to want something more from life. To my kids, you may not know it, but you make me intrinsically happy and proud and let me see the joy in life's simple events on a daily basis. I would like to thank my aunt Susan, who helped me get through all of the rough patches in life. I would like thank my priest, Father Cyril Edwards, for planting seeds in my head which grew into trees of wisdom. I would like to thank all of my deceased relatives and pets, especially 318. You may not be physically here, but your presence is revealed to me daily, and you give me hope. Lastly, I would like to thank the shows *Ancient Aliens* from the History channel, in particular Erich von Daniken and Giorgio Tsoukalos, and *Lucifer* from Fox network because these shows made me think, what if?

ABOUT THE AUTHOR

I am a thirty-eight-year-old pharmacist. I have been married for over five years now and have a three-year-old son and a fifteen-year-old stepdaughter. I have been divorced once and was an alcoholic for about twelve years. I have traveled to many countries but have lived on the same block for my entire life. I am a Roman Catholic and am a very spiritual person but not necessarily sold on all aspects of religion. I have many pets, including rabbits, an iguana, numerous fish, three dogs, and a cat. I support the humane society for animals and have rescued my rabbits and one of my dogs (deceased, 2015) from there. I rescued my cat from the street.

I do not read books and rarely use social media. I watch all sorts of TV and love movies and sports. I enjoy playing sports, exercising, hunting, fishing, and enjoying nature. I graduated magna cum laude from both the University of Scranton and Wilkes University. I have a bachelor's degree in biology and a doctorate degree in pharmacy.

All ideas which I have included in this book were developed by me, and originally for me, through inspiration from many of life's tragedies, triumphs, and daily events. I needed a way to explain life without accepting ideas blindly. If something is true, I needed to know why it is true. Sometimes inspiration came from TV shows, sometimes it came from quiet reflection, and sometimes it came from lifelong analysis of patterns and behaviors. Whatever the case, all ideas in this book were not taken from any other author or organization, as I don't read books, blogs, or social media and I don't belong to any groups or associations.

CPSIA information can be obtained
at www.ICGtesting.com
Printed in the USA
LVOW11s1056030117

519549LV00001B/116/P